The Wall Street Bombing of 1920: The History and Anarchist Attack on New York City

By Charles River Editors

A picture of the explosion's aftermath

About Charles River Editors

Charles River Editors provides superior editing and original writing services across the digital publishing industry, with the expertise to create digital content for publishers across a vast range of subject matter. In addition to providing original digital content for third party publishers, we also republish civilization's greatest literary works, bringing them to new generations of readers via ebooks.

Sign up here to receive updates about free books as we publish them, and visit Our Kindle Author Page to browse today's free promotions and our most recently published Kindle titles.

Introduction

"As an anarchist, I am opposed to violence. But if the people want to do away with assassins, they must do away with the conditions which produce murderers." – Emma Goldman

One September day, New York City suffered a devastating act of domestic terrorism, but that day was not the 11th, and the attack took place over 80 years before the most notorious terrorist attack on America. In 1920, an explosion in the Financial District of New York City killed 38 people, injured hundreds more, and caused damage that is still visible on some of Wall Street's most famous buildings today. Although the attack has largely been forgotten, in terms of casualties, it was the worst act of terrorism in the United States until the bombing in Oklahoma City conducted by Timothy McVeigh in 1995.

The investigation into the bombing involved 10 government agencies and extended across the world, yet after three years of intensive work, investigators were finally forced to admit that they had no idea who had planted the bomb. Subsequent investigations have uncovered many suspects, but no one was ever charged with offenses related to the explosion, even as suspicions have always fallen on anarchists, political activists who sought revolutionary change.

By 1920, the end of World War I had swept away the seeming stability of the pre-war world. In Europe, the Austro-Hungarian Empire fragmented into new nation states, Imperial Germany was replaced first by a Communist state and then by the democratic Weimar Republic, and Italy was brought close to complete economic collapse and riven by divisions between those who wanted to see the replacement of the current regime with a Communist state and those who struggled to enforce the status quo. Britain and France, though victorious, were crippled by the costs of the war, both economically and in terms of huge numbers of casualties. America emerged, for the first time, as a world power.

However, it was in Russia that the greatest changes were taking place. Though the October Revolution in 1917 is generally celebrated as the beginning of Communist control in Russia, in 1920 a bitter civil war was being fought between the "Red" supporters of Vladimir Lenin's Soviet Union and "White" forces who demanded the return of the tsar and the end of the fledgling Communist state. What is now often forgotten is that large numbers of American, British, and French troops fought on the side of the White forces, attempting to remove the Communist regime and to prevent the spread of Communism outside Russia. In fact, in 1920, an American Expeditionary Force controlled large parts of Siberia and occupied the city of Vladivostok.

The end of the horrors of the Great War, the "war to end all wars," seemed to presage the end of conflict itself, and for many people, Communism seemed to offer something genuinely new and different, a real alternative to capitalism based not on the creation of wealth but the sharing of control of the resources of a nation with its people. Supporters extolled the virtues of Communism with evangelical zeal, claiming that the new system would quickly spread around the world. Countries such as America, Britain, and France were viewed as being opposed to change in general and to Communism specifically. Many countries also saw the rise of "anarchist" movements, sometimes affiliated with the Communist cause and sometimes pursuing their own quite separate vision of a people's Utopia. The one thing that all those who sought change agreed on was that this could only come when capitalism and the social, political, and democratic systems that underpinned it were removed. Some pursued this vision of the future through political action. Others used violence.

In America, which had large immigrant communities, these movements gained increasing numbers of followers, so when a bomb exploded on Wall Street, the heart of the American financial system, it was perhaps natural that suspicions immediately fell on anarchist movements. Was this an attempt to destabilize capitalism in America or even to assassinate leading figures in the financial world? Finding clear answers to those questions proved beyond the capacity of the agencies tasked with investigating the bombing. Even now, there is no certain answer as to who planted the Wall Street bomb, but it has long been attributed to anarchists.

The Wall Street Bombing of 1920: The History and Legacy of the Notorious Anarchist Attack on New York City looks at the political background of 20th century America, the mysteries behind the attack, and its impact. Along with pictures of important people, places, and events, you will learn about the Wall Street Bombing like never before.

The Wall Street Bombing of 1920: The History and Legacy of the Notorious Anarchist Attack on New York City

A New Manifesto

In 1848 two German political philosophers, Karl Marx and Friedrich Engels, published what in retrospect has become seen as one of the most important and influential political documents ever written; Manifest der Kommunistischen Partei (Manifesto of the Communist Party). This was an analysis of society, especially capitalist society, in terms of class. The manifesto argued that the current situation, with growing industrialization causing wealth to be concentrated in the hands of a small number of people while the majority lived in poverty, was not only unacceptable and unfair, it was a situation that could not continue.

Marx

Engels

Marx and Engels argued that the bourgeoisie, the people who owned the means of production, would be overthrown by the lower classes, the proletariat, who would establish a form of government where industry was controlled not by private individuals but by the state on behalf of the people. The result would be a classless society where everything was owned by the people and shared equally. However, the *Communist Manifesto* was much more than a scholarly dissection of what was wrong with mid-19th century society, it was a call to action, perhaps even to revolution to establish this Utopian vision of a new society. It ended with the stirring words, "Working Men of All Countries, Unite!"

The new philosophy described by Marx and Engels quickly found many adherents. Industrialization in Europe and elsewhere had changed the nature of many societies. Where in the eighteenth century many countries had been mainly agrarian with a relatively small manufacturing capacity dominated by skilled workers, by the mid-19th century the increasing use of machines for manufacture meant the widespread use of unskilled workers who could be paid low wages. Wealth became concentrated in the hands of the people who owned factories while the bulk of the working class lived in poverty.

The same year that the manifesto was published, many of the countries of Europe were convulsed by popular uprisings in what became known as the Springtime of the Peoples. Mass demonstrations and even attempts at armed uprisings affected France, Italy, the Netherlands, Denmark, the Austro-Hungarian Empire and Prussia and the other states that would become the German Empire. Tens of thousands of people were killed as a direct result of uprisings in the summer of 1848 and many more were imprisoned or exiled. This wave of revolutionary fervor led to little permanent change, but it seemed to confirm what Marx and Engels were saying: that the proletariat were no longer willing to accept their poverty and were willing to take violent action to change things.

For many people, and not just members of the proletariat, the ideas put forth in the *Communist Manifesto* seemed like the only logical route to a fairer, more equable society. Many seemed to accept that revolution and violence were the only routes to lasting and significant change. Several movements in Europe were directly influenced by the manifesto with perhaps the best-known example being when Communist rebels, the Communards, seized the city of Paris in 1871 and held it for two months before a bloody suppression by the French Army.

In Russia, where serfdom was only abolished in 1861, the ideas of Marx and Engels were planted in fertile soil. A number of Communist revolutionary secret societies emerged and in 1881 the tsar, Alexander II, was assassinated by a member of one such group, *Narodnaya Volya* ("People's Will"). By the beginning of the 20th century, the ideas and ideals of Communism had spread around the world. The horrors of World War I only seemed to increase the desire for a new form of society and in 1917, Russia became the first European monarchy to be overthrown by a Communist uprising. In the chaos following the end of the war in 1918, Germany, Austria and Italy all teetered on the edge of revolution. It seemed that Communism's moment had finally arrived.

However, from the very beginning, there were some people who disagreed with Marx and Engels, not about the need for a new type of society but about the way in which this should be achieved. In general, Marx and Engels favored change through agitation, education, and electoral reform rather than violent uprising. To them and to many others it seemed obvious that if universal suffrage were to be achieved, then the fact that the proletariat overwhelmingly outnumbered the bourgeoisie meant that radical change would inevitably follow.

However, even within the emerging Communist Party, there were those who disagreed. While the "specter of Communism" terrified those with wealth and in positions of power, some felt that the ideas of Marx and Engels were not sufficiently radical. One such person was Mikhail Alexandrovich Bakunin, a Russian revolutionary who initially supported the *Communist Manifesto*, but soon became disenchanted with it. He felt, with some prescience, that the kind of state described by the *Communist Manifesto* would become not a nation run on behalf of its people but a dictatorship operated on behalf of the party. In 1872, Bakunin's disagreements with Marx led to his being expelled from the International Working Men's Association, the main International Communist group. Bakunin went on to write a number of influential books and papers before his death in 1876, which led to the appearance of a new movement: the anarchists.

Bakunin

Unlike Communism, the anarchist movement did not have a central document comparable to the *Communist Manifesto*, and there were a number of competing factions including anarcho-collectivism, anarcho-communism, anarcho-syndicalism and individualist anarchism. Each had one thing in common: they sought the complete abolition of Nation States and the establishment of a new form of society where individuals were free from control or coercion.

Anarchism found enthusiastic followers in Europe, especially in France and Italy, but it also flourished in the United States. When the American Civil War ended in 1865, American industrial capacity was large, but comprised mainly of small businesses using manual labor and limited technology. In the 30 years from 1870–1900, this changed dramatically. Industrialization, particularly the widespread use of machines to speed production, led to the manufacture of many, many new products which were distributed to a mass-market via the growing railroad network.

Especially in the North, people moved to cities to find work in factories. In 1870, only around 25% of the population of America lived in urban areas but by 1916, this had risen to 50%. A tidal wave of immigrants provided yet more labor as well as a market for the products produced in the new factories – between 1870 and 1916, the population of America grew from around forty million people to over one hundred million with the bulk of the increase due to new arrivals from Europe.

However, industrialization also changed the nature of the workforce in America. Most factories did not need skilled workers, they required only "machine minders," low-skilled workers paid as little as possible. American society changed too. A very small number of people, mainly those who owned the factories and the financiers who supported them, became staggeringly, absurdly wealthy. When financier J.P. Morgan died in 1913, he left an estate worth $80 million. At that time, the average skilled worker received less than $20 per week in wages, but upon hearing of the amount he had left, billionaire John D. Rockefeller remarked of Morgan, "And to think he wasn't even a rich man!"

Below the ranks of the unbelievably rich, there was a small middle class, mainly small business owners and those who managed factories and manufacturing and distribution centers. However, at the bottom of the pile was a huge population of the working class who often existing in abject poverty. These people, who worked in the most menial and dangerous jobs, made less than $12 for a back-breaking, 60-hour work week. The influx of immigrants meant that unemployment was high, which kept wages down. While Rockefeller might have quipped that $80 million did not even qualify as "rich," the majority of people in America were living in squalid conditions where they struggled to find sufficient money each week to pay for a place to live and enough to eat.

Unsurprisingly, a number of movements dedicated to reform and a more equable distribution of wealth developed in America in the late 1800s. Unions began to emerge and organized the first strikes. Members of the clergy, social reformers and others were so disgusted by the squalid living conditions in many American cities that they formed a new political party, the Populist Party, to campaign on behalf of the poorest people in America.

At the same time, some people advocated not reform but violent revolution. In the last decades of the 19th century and first decades of the 20th century, what people would now call terrorism became a feature of American life. Bombs were sent in the mail to mayors and important industrialists and dynamite was used to destroy railroad lines and factories. There were attempts to assassinate not just governors and judges but also important industrialists. For example, financier and industrialist Henry Clay Frick was shot by a leading member of the American anarchist movement, Alexander Berkman, in 1892. Even the president was not safe – in September 1901, President William McKinley was shot and fatally wounded by an anarchist named Leon Czolgosz.

Meanwhile, Chicago, a city with a large population of immigrants from European countries, became the center of the anarchist movement in America. On May 1, 1886, strikes were called in a number of American cities, and a number of anarchists were involved in violent protests that followed, and although it's no longer well known as a flashpoint, few things were as controversial during the late 19th century as the Haymarket Affair. Depending on one's perspective, the riots and the violence that ensued were the result of anarchist terrorists attacking law enforcement authorities with a homemade bomb that was detonated during a large public event, killing a police officer and wounding several more. Others who were more sympathetic to the plight of the people protesting for better working conditions that night in Haymarket Square in Chicago on May 4, 1886 portray it as a peaceful rally that was marred by a heavy handed response attempting to disperse the protesters.

What is clear is that the moments following the explosion were characterized by confusion and bedlam, as some people ran away and others ran toward the site. By the time the shooting was done, nearly a dozen lay dead, including a number of police officers, and makeshift hospitals were soon overwhelmed. Citizens in the area began to cry out for justice, and police detectives poured through the city, making arrests and questioning thousands. As word spread about the attack, cities around the country went on high alert, concerned that they could be next. It was soon determined that a traditionally anti-American group was responsible for the attack, and many threatened mob violence against anyone who looked like they might be involved with the group. The press egged on those in the public with cries for revenge and justice. Eventually, the suspected perpetrators' trial began, a sensational event followed closely by many across the nation. Tensions ran high as those involved were prosecuted and defended, and when the jury convicted 8 anarchists of conspiracy and some of them were sentenced to death, many rejoiced while others cried out that Lady Justice had miscarried the case.

Lost amidst the violence was the fact that the protests that culminated with the Haymarket Affair had come in response to previous labor strikes across the country, and controversial police shootings of some workers on strike, which took on a discriminatory undertone because many of the laborers were immigrants facing poor working conditions. It was against this backdrop that political anarchists also got involved, which muddled things and ultimately brought blowback against immigrant communities after the Haymarket Affair.

More importantly, workers and those advocating on their behalf were galvanized by the events to push for what they considered much needed reforms, many of which would come over the next few decades. As professor William J. Adelman put it, "No single event has influenced the history of labor in Illinois, the United States, and even the world, more than the Chicago Haymarket Affair. It began with a rally on May 4, 1886, but the consequences are still being felt today." Chicago has since commemorated both the workers and the police with various memorials and plaques.

A contemporary engraving of the Haymarket Affair

The Rise of Political Violence

By the early years of the 20th century, anarchism had become widely accepted as a more radical alternative to Communism. In 1907, the International Anarchist Congress of Amsterdam attracted delegates from most European countries, as well as Japan, the United States and a number of South and Central American countries. But by then, many members of the anarchist movement had become convinced that the only route to real change lay in the "propaganda of the deed," acts of political violence intended to destabilize the state and encourage the mass of people to violent uprising. This stemmed directly from the ideas of Bakunin, who in 1870 had written, "We must spread our principles, not with words but with deeds, for this is the most popular, the most potent, and the most irresistible form of propaganda."[1]

To Communists, this was a counterproductive strategy, as they felt that small-scale acts of violence were unlikely to achieve significant change and would instead bring about repression by the state that would make revolution more difficult. But to many anarchists, the meaning of propaganda of the deed was clear, and it motivated them to attack members of the government and those who supported and maintained the capitalist society.

---

[1] Bakunin, M., *Letter to a Frenchman on the Present Crisis*, 1870.

One such man in America was Johann Most. Johann Joseph "Hans" Most was born in Bavaria in 1846 and was an early enthusiast of the ideas of Marx and Engels, but he soon became more interested in the anarchist ideology of Bakunin. In 1874, Most was elected as a Social Democratic deputy to the German Reichstag, but his impassioned speeches on the need for revolution and the use of violence to achieve that led to him being expelled from Germany in 1878. He moved first to France, but he was expelled from that country later the same year, so he then moved to Britain and started an anarchist newspaper, *Freiheit* ("Freedom"). His enthusiastic support for the assassination of Tsar Alexander II in 1881 and his suggestion that the assassination of monarchs be repeated in other European countries led to his imprisonment in Britain and his expulsion from that country when he was released in 1882. Most emigrated to America and arrived in New York City later the same year.

Most

Most began giving political speeches almost as soon as he arrived in America, and within a short time, he had relaunched *Freiheit* as a German language newspaper in America. He also joined the Social Revolutionary Club, an anarchist association based in New York. Most understood that the lack of an aristocracy in America did not mean that there was not a class system, and the office from which he published Freiheit was just a few blocks from Wall Street, which he soon came to see as the center for the repression of workers in America. He wrote in an editorial, "In America the place of the monarchs is filled by monopolists. The sovereignty of the people falls prostrate into the dust before the influence of these money kings, railroad magnates, coal barons and factory lords."

To Most, the solution was simple: these people should be killed, and in such an obvious and public way as to encourage others to do the same. In 1884, Most took a job (using an assumed name) in a dynamite factory in Jersey City so that he could learn about explosives and in particular about dynamite. As a result of what he learned, in 1885 he published a pamphlet, snappily titled "The Science of Revolutionary Warfare: A Handbook of Instruction Regarding the Use and Manufacture of Nitroglycerine, Dynamite, Gun-Cotton, Fulminating Mercury, Bombs, Arsons, Poisons, Etc." The contents of this booklet were as explosive as the materials it described. It told readers how and where to steal explosives, and how much dynamite should be used to blow up structures of various sizes. For small structures, 10 pounds was deemed sufficient, but for large churches, military, and government buildings, as much as 50 pounds might be required.

This was combined with increasingly violent political rhetoric from Most. In 1885, he wrote, "The existing system will be quickest and most radically overthrown by the annihilation of its exponents. Therefore, massacres of the enemies of the people must be set in motion."[2]

Inevitably, Most eventually came to the attention of American authorities. He was arrested and imprisoned for short periods in 1886, 1887, and again in 1902 after claiming in an editorial in *Freiheit* that the assassination of President McKinley could not be considered a crime. At the same time, the angry rhetoric of Most and other anarchists encouraged a wave of violence in the last decades of the 19th century, though this was centered in Europe rather than America. Bombs were planted and thrown, political leaders and royalty were assassinated in Spain, France, Austria and Italy, and many anarchists were arrested in the aftermath.

In America, there was discussion of banning known anarchists from emigrating, but nothing concrete was done before President McKinley was assassinated by a young anarchist, Leon Czolgosz. Czolgosz later claimed that he had been inspired to commit the murder after attending a lecture by Emma Goldman, one of Most's enthusiastic supporters, and many American anarchists saw the assassination of the president as a triumphant vindication of the policy of propaganda by deed. One month after the event, Goldman wrote, ""Never before in the history of governments has the sound of a pistol shot so startled, terrorized, and horrified the self-satisfied, indifferent, contented, and indolent public, as has the one fired by Leon Czolgosz when he struck down William McKinley, president of the money kings and trust magnates of this country."[3]

---

[2] Ketcham, C., *When Revolution Came to America*, 2014.
[3] Emma Goldman, *The Tragedy at Buffalo*, Free Society, Oct. 6, 1901.

Goldman

Czolgosz

Leon Czolgosz was executed in October 1901 and his body dissolved in acid to prevent his grave becoming a focal point for anarchists. The new president, Teddy Roosevelt, himself something of a populist, declared, "The anarchist, and especially the anarchist in the United States, is merely one type of criminal, more dangerous than any other because he represents the same depravity in a greater degree. The man who advocates anarchy directly or indirectly, in any shape or fashion, or the man who apologizes for anarchists and their deeds, makes himself morally accessory to murder before the fact. The anarchist is a criminal whose perverted instincts lead him to prefer confusion and chaos to the most beneficent form of social order. His protest of concern for workingmen is outrageous in its impudent falsity; for if the political institutions of this country do not afford opportunity to every honest and intelligent son of toil, then the door of hope is forever closed against him. The anarchist is everywhere not merely the enemy of system and of progress, but the deadly foe of liberty. If ever anarchy is triumphant, its triumph will last for but one red moment, to be succeeded, for ages by the gloomy night of despotism."

In 1902, individual states began passing legislation that banned speeches or writing that encouraged acts of violence against the government, and in 1903, Congress passed new legislation that prevented the immigration of any person to the United States who "[d]isbelieves in or who is opposed to all organized government . . . or who advocates or teaches the duty, necessity, or propriety of the unlawful assaulting or killing of any officer . . . of the Government of the United States."

Despite these moves, violence continued. In December 1905, Idaho's Governor Frank Steunenberg was killed when a bomb planted on the gate to his home exploded. Harry Orchard, a former member of the Western Federation of Miners (WFM), a radical labor union, was charged with the murder. At the trial, he claimed that members of the WFM, including Bill Haywood, the Union Secretary, had paid him to carry out the assassination. Orchard was found guilty, but Haywood was acquitted. Following his acquittal, Haywood became the center of a growing radical movement in America, and in 1905 he was part of a group that founded The Industrial Workers of the World (IWW), an even more radical international labor union whose members became known as "wobblies."

Steunenberg

By 1908, explosions on streetcars, bridges and dams had become almost commonplace in America, and since most were related to labor disputes, many people connected them to both the IWW and the anarchist movement. In 1910 an explosion ripped apart the offices of the *Los Angeles Times* in downtown Los Angeles, killing 21 people. A subsequent investigation discovered another bomb in the home of Harrison Gray Otis, the owner of the newspaper and an outspoken critic of labor unions.

In July 1914, three men were killed in an explosion at an apartment on New York City's prestigious Lexington Avenue, and all three men were discovered to be anarchists who had been attempting to plant a bomb in the apartment of John D. Rockefeller, Jr. Over the next year, there were a series of explosions in New York, targeting churches, courthouses, and police buildings. These caused relatively little damage and no fatalities, but all were generally assumed to be the work of anarchists. This seemed to be confirmed in February 1915 when two Italian anarchists, Frank Abarno and Carmine Carbone, were caught while attempting to plant a bomb in St. Patrick's Cathedral.

In February 1916, a bomb exploded amongst a crowd taking part in a parade in San Francisco, killing 10 people and injuring more than 40. Soon after, police arrested several anarchists accused of planting the bomb.

The Bureau of Investigation and the Palmer Raids

Although the police frequently caught suspects, they seemed powerless to prevent the planting of bombs, both by anarchists and increasingly by saboteurs sent by Germany to undermine American industrial capacity during World war I. What was needed, it seemed to many, was an agency capable of carrying out investigations across the country and specifically intended to counter domestic terrorism.

President Roosevelt initially asked Congress to form a federal detective force in 1907, but his request was denied, as many members of Congress and the general public were opposed to the formation of such a force, fearing that it would become a kind of secret police. There was also the fear that the creation of such a group would increase federal power, something that many felt was in opposition to the Constitution, which specifically limited federal power in terms of direct governance. However, existing police forces seemed unable to deal with anarchist terror attacks, and the groups that carried these out often spanned several states, causing jurisdiction problems for detectives investigating the groups themselves or acts of terror. Manpower was also limited to state detective forces, so important cases were often contracted out to private detective agencies such as the Pinkertons.

When it had conducted investigations in the past, the Department of Justice had been forced to borrow Secret Service operatives from the Treasury, but in early 1908, Congress passed a bill prohibiting the use of Secret Service staff by other agencies. Thus, in July 1908, President Roosevelt ordered Attorney General Charles Bonaparte to create a federal detective force within the Department of Justice.

In July 1908, a group of 34 agents was formed under the leadership of Chief Examiner Stanley W. Finch of the Department of Justice. Initially the group was known as the Office of the Chief Examiner, but within one year it was renamed the Bureau of Investigation (BOI) by Attorney General George W. Wickersham. Initially, the Bureau had been involved in investigating interstate prostitution and antitrust cases but during World War I its role expanded to enforcing draft laws and finding those who sought to avoid serving in the U.S. Military as well as hunting German spies and saboteurs.

Finch

At the end of the war, there was some discussion about just what the role of the Bureau should be, but a wave of anarchist bombings in the first half of 1919 seemed to provide the logical answer. By this time, the Bolshevik Revolution had spread throughout Central Europe and seemed to threaten the rest of the world. In America, newspaper stories openly worried about a similar revolution in the country. A rash of strikes fed fears that class warfare, fomented by foreign communist forces, would break out at any moment. As a result, the BOI, established in 1905 to investigate federal crimes, was turned against left wing organizations such as the anti-war Socialist Party of America and the Industrial Workers of the World. Leaders of these groups such as socialist Eugene Debs were prosecuted under the Espionage Act of 1917, which made it a crime to interfere with military operations, and the Sedition Act of 1918, which forbade the use of "disloyal, profane, scurrilous, or abusive language" about the United States government, flag, or armed forces of the United States during wartime. These measures, along with the Immigration Act of 1918, which targeted a variety of radicals, provided the government with a potent means of targeting the new threats even after the war was over.

On February 2, 1919, 35,000 shipyard workers in Seattle went on strike to demand wage increases, and they appealed to the Seattle Central Labor Council for support. Their appeal was met with widespread enthusiasm from other unions, and within two weeks other local unions banded together to call for a general strike to begin on February 6. According to later testimony, it appears that some of the workers were motivated by propaganda concerning the events in the new Soviet Union. A Seattle labor leader said of workers' politics in June 1919, "I believe that 95 percent of us agree that the workers should control the industries. Nearly all of us agree on that but very strenuously disagree on the method. Some of us think we can get control through the Cooperative movement, some of us think through political action, and others think through industrial action."

A picture of the Seattle General Strike

A journalist reported on the spread of propaganda related to the Russian Revolution, "For some time these pamphlets were seen by hundreds on Seattle's streetcars and ferries, read by men of the shipyards on their way to work. Seattle's businessmen commented on the phenomenon sourly; it was plain to everyone that these workers were conscientiously and energetically studying how to organize their coming to power. Already, workers in Seattle talked about "workers' power" as a practical policy for the not far distant future."

The rhetoric of the strikers amplified the fears of Americans over a possible revolution, even as the general strike itself collapsed, ending on February 11 after the Seattle General Strike Committee acceded to pressure from the American Federation of Labor (AFL) and international labor organizations and voted to end the strike. The Committee stated, "Pressure from international officers of unions, from executive committees of unions, from the 'leaders' in the labor movement, even from those very leaders who are still called 'Bolsheviki' by the undiscriminating press. And, added to all these, the pressure upon the workers themselves, not of the loss of their own jobs, but of living in a city so tightly closed."

The general strike made a national celebrity of Seattle Mayor Ole Hanson, who took credit for ending the strike. Resigning a few months later, Hanson traveled the country speaking of the dangers of "domestic Bolshevism" and amplifying the perception of the general strike as a revolutionary event.

In the wake of the strike, a subcommittee of the Senate Judiciary Committee chaired by Senator Lee Slater Overman of North Carolina, which had been formed to investigate the influence of German propaganda, expanded its investigations into the influence of Bolshevism in the United States. Senate Resolution 439, proposed by Senator Thomas J. Walsh and passed unanimously, called on the Overman Committee to investigate "any efforts being made to propagate in this country the principles of any party exercising or claiming to exercise any authority in Russia" and "any effort to incite the overthrow of the Government of this country."

Overman

The Committee conducted a month's worth of hearings, beginning on February 11 (the day the Seattle General Strike ended) and ending on March 10, 1919. The Committee called over two dozen witnesses, mostly anti-Bolshevik activists and Russian refugees who had left during the Russian Revolution. They described in lurid detail the terrors perpetrated in the Soviet Union and warned in stark terms about what could happen in the United States should the country have its own revolution. Other witnesses warned against radical professors in colleges and universities spreading revolutionary thoughts among the nation's youth, the role of Jews in communist organizations, and radical ideas concerning women. All focused on the threat posed by immigrants, in particular from South and Eastern Europe, in spreading socialism, communism, and anarchy.

The Committee released a 35,000-word final report in June 1919, which in hindsight was notable for its utter lack of documentation of a domestic threat from communist revolutionaries and other radicals. Instead, it offered a list of conditions in the Soviet Union and the policies advanced by the new Soviet rulers, trying to draw some connection between them and the positions of American radicals. For example, in discussing the Constitution of the Soviet Union, the report warned, "The investigation which your committee has conducted convinces it that few of either the advocates or opponents, in this country, of the present Russian Socialist Federated Soviet Republic are familiar with the fundamental principles upon which this Government is attempting to perpetuate itself. Consequently the agitation growing out of developments in Russia has largely degenerated into appeals to the prejudices and the animosities that are inherent in the selfish natures of most individuals and little or no appeal has been made to the intelligence of the people. It is therefore not surprising that the word 'Bolshevism' has now become merely a generic term, and in America is nothing more than a slogan of the elements of unrest and discontent."

As a result of its hearings, the report made several recommendations for legislation to counteract the threats they outlined. To limit the influence of radical newspapers in both English and foreign languages, the report proposed that Congress pass a law that would allow the public to be "afforded an ample opportunity to know just who their instructors are." Legislation was proposed that would particularly target immigrants, who were seen as the main source of the radical threat. According to the report's authors, "Foreign-language newspapers are a danger to the country unless they are utilized to assist in the assimilation of the alien element and to aid in the process of Americanization which is essential to the healthy development the population into a homogeneous whole. This much-sought-for Americanization would be impeded by either depriving the alien of the educational value of a newspaper in the only language he can read or by withholding from him proper aid and facility for learning the English language and failing to encourage him to acquire the educational advantages incident to the mastering of the language of his adopted country. With this in mind, therefore, this committee recommends legislation to control and regulate the printing of foreign-language publications in this country."

The report also warned against the "forces of anarchy and violence...utilizing the financial resources plundered by them from the European people...to import into this country money, literature, and hired agents for the purpose of promulgating the doctrine of force, violence, assassination, confiscation, and revolution...As an effect of these activities there has appeared in this country a large group of persons who advocate the overthrow of all organized government, and especially the Government of the United States, who favor revolutionary movements, repudiate the Constitution of the United States, and refuse to respect our national emblem and our governmental institutions. There are found among the leaders of this group many aliens who unhesitatingly use the hospitality which this country has extended to them and who because of that leadership are able to retard the real americanization of the more ignorant residents possessing similar racial characteristics. These persons encourage and maintain a solidarity of the people of the several foreign tongues which is used to create and incite a class hatred that is quickly absorbed by and incorporated into the revolutionary movement led by them. The alien element in this country is the most susceptible and is the first to adopt violence as an effective weapon for supremacy."

For all of the fears raised by the committee about the potential for Bolshevik-inspired violent revolution, when actual radical violence occurred, it was inspired not by the Soviet Union but carried out by an Italian anarchist. Sometime in late April 1919, booby-trapped packages containing dynamite bombs were mailed to 36 prominent political and business leaders, including Attorney General A. Mitchell Palmer. The bombs were sent by followers of the Italian anarchist Luigi Galleani, who was an enthusiastic advocate of the doctrine of "propaganda of the deed," the use of violence to eliminate those he viewed as tyrants and oppressors and to act as a catalyst to overthrow the existing government. His followers intended for the bombs to be delivered on May Day, since May 1 has been celebrated since the founding of the Second International in 1890 as a day of solidarity among communists, anarchists, and social revolutionaries.

Galleani

Palmer

The mail bombs were wrapped in brown paper and had similar address and advertising labels. Inside the brown paper wrapping was a box wrapped in bright green paper and stamped "Gimble Brothers-Novelty Samples." The box contained a six inch by three inch block of hollowed-out wood stuffed with a stick of dynamite, and fastened to the wood block was a fuse consisting of a small vial of sulfuric acid and three blasting caps. Opening the box would trigger the bomb by tripping a spring at one end of the box.

The *Chicago Tribune* reported, "Six of these deadly messengers reached their destination. One of them exploded when opened. I wounded the wife of former Senator Hardwick of Georgia and her maid...Agents of the department of justice said they believed the mailing of the bombs was timed to cause a reign of terror on May day, observed throughout the world not only by peaceful labor organizations, but by the most pronounced radicals...It was apparent the makers of the bombs hoped to exterminate every one who has been prominently involved in the prosecution or deportation of members of the I.W.W. [International Workers of the World] and other radicals. Not only were officers of the immigration bureau marked for destruction but also the authors of the bill which would have stopped immigration for a year. This measure would have made it difficult for alien radicals to gain access to this country."

The *Tribune* report referred to Senator Thomas Hardwick, a co-sponsor of the Immigration Act of 1918, which made it easier for the government to deport anarchists, communists, labor organizers and other activists. The bomb blew off the hands of Hardwick's housekeeper when she opened the package, and it injured Hardwick's wife.

One of the six individuals who received bombs was Judge Kenesaw Mountain Landis, who presided over the Chicago trial of members of the Industrial Workers of the World in 1918. The *Tribune* reported, "Mailman Sam Kaminsky threw a parcel over the transom into the chambers of Federal Judge Landis at the federal building yesterday morning. Ben Stern, a clerk, stumbled over it as he entered the office and tossed it on the desk of Miss Hilda Krekel, the secretary. Miss Krekel used it all day as a paper weight. Newspaper reporters, late in the afternoon, discovered the package and called in Gen. James E. Stuart, chief of post office inspectors. The inspector examined the wrapper and postmarks and said it was, beyond any question, one of the infernal machines being sent broadcast from New York to the country's leading officials."

Landis

In addition to Landis and Hardwick, others who received bombs were San Francisco District Attorney Charles Fickert, his assistant Edward Cunha, Alabama Congressman John L. Burnett, and former Seattle Mayor Ole Hanson. In addition to Palmer, others who had bombs addressed to them that were intercepted in the mail included John D. Rockefeller, J.P. Morgan, Commissioner of Immigration Anthony Caminetti, Secretary of Labor William B. Wilson, Supreme Court Justice Oliver Wendell Holmes, New York Mayor John F. Hylan, and Pennsylvania Governor William C. Sproul. The one person of no national prominence to have a bomb addressed to them was Rayme Weston Finch, a field agent with the Department of Justice's Bureau of Investigation. In 1918, he had arrested two prominent Galleanists while leading a raid on the Galleanist publication *Cronaca Sovversiva*.

Wilson

These latter bombs did not reach their intended targets primarily because they lacked sufficient postage, prompting a Justice Department official to comment, "The sender of the infernal machines lacks cunning. I believe they are sent by an insane crank, not smart enough to use different wrappers or to make sure the postage is sufficient." Remarkably, no one was killed in these April attacks.

The Galleanists struck again on the evening of June 2, 1919. On that date, the anarchists detonated nine bombs in eight cities almost simultaneously. The bombs were much larger than the April devices, consisting of 25 pounds of dynamite packages with heavy metal slugs meant to act as shrapnel. The bombs were mainly addressed to government officials who had endorsed the deportation of radicals or participated in the prosecution of suspected anarchists. Delivered along with the bombs was a flyer titled, "Plain Words," which said in part:

> "The powers that be make no secret of their will to stop, here in America, the world-wide spread of revolution. The powers that be must reckon that they will have to accept the fight they have provoked.

> "A time when the social question's solution can be delayed no longer; class war is on and can not cease but with a complete victory for the International proletariat.

> "The challenge is an old one, oh "democratic" lords of the autocratic republic. We have been dreaming of freedom, we have talked of liberty, we have aspired to a better world, and you jailed us, you clubbed us, you deported us, you murdered us whenever you could...

> "It is history of yesterday that your gunmen were shooting and murdering unarmed masses by the wholesale; it has been the history of every day in your regime; and now all prospects are even worse.

> "Do not expect us to sit down and pray and cry. We accept your challenges and mean to stick to our war duties. We know that all you do is for your defense as a class; we know also that the proletariat has the same right to protect itself, since their press has been suffocated, their mouths muzzled; we mean to speak for them the voice of dynamite, through the mouth of guns...

> "We are not many, perhaps more than you dream of, though but are all determined to fight to the last, till a man remains buried in your Bastilles, till a hostage of the working class is left to the tortures of your police system, and will never rest until your fall is complete, and the laboring masses have taken possession of all that rightly belongs to them.

> "There will be bloodshed; we will not dodge; there will have to be murder: we will kill, because it is necessary; there will have to be destruction; we will destroy to rid the world of your tyrannical institutions...

"Do not seek to believe that we are the Germans' or the devil's paid agents; you know well we are class-conscious men with strong determination, and no vulgar liability. And never hope that your cops, and your hounds will ever succeed in ridding the country of the anarchistic germ that pulses in our veins.

We know how we stand with you and know how to take care of ourselves. Besides, you will never get all of us * * * and we multiply nowadays. Just wait and resign to your fate, since privilege and riches have turned your heads.

"Long live social revolution! Down with tyranny!"

As in April, Palmer was a target, and this time, the bomb meant for Palmer took the life of Carlo Valdinoci. A former editor of *Cronaca Sovversiva* and a close associate of Galleani, Valdinoci died when the bomb exploded prematurely.

Others who escaped personal injury, but sustained some to their dwelling, were Palmer's neighbors, Franklin D. Roosevelt and his wife Eleanor. According to Roosevelt's account in the *New York Times*, the windows of his residence were blown in, and even worse, a part of a body (later proven to be part of the bomber Valdinoci) was blown across the street from Palmer's house and landed on Roosevelt's doorstep. So powerful was the bomb that homes up and down R Street sustained damage. In addition to Valdinoci, a bomb in New York killed a night watchman, William Boehner

It was clear that the anarchists were back and operating across the United States. When in June 1919 Attorney General Palmer appointed a new Director of the Bureau of Investigation, William James Flynn, he made it clear where he thought the Bureau should focus its attention, calling the new Director "[t]he leading, organizing detective of America... Flynn is an anarchist chaser... the greatest anarchist expert in the United States."

Flynn

Investigators began almost immediately to hunt for the bombers. The only real clue they had was the flyer, which they traced to a printing shop owned by two anarchists, typesetter Andrea Salsedo and compositor Roberto Elia, both Galleanists. Salsedo committed suicide, and there was insufficient evidence to try Elia for involvement in the bombings. Elia refused to testify about his role in return for a cancellation of deportation proceedings against him. No one was ever tried for the bombings.

While the anarchist's bombs failed to kill any of their intended targets, they succeeded in further increasing the Red Scare hysteria in the country, and other events in the summer of 1919 fed a paranoia about an organized Bolshevik conspiracy intent on revolution. On May 1, 1919, the normally peaceful May Day parades turned violent when large crowds of leftists were met by police and groups of self-described patriots intent on breaking up the demonstrations. The *New York Times* described incidents around the country of violence associated with May Day. In New York, the paper reported, "Soldiers and Sailors invaded several of the meeting places and broke up the gatherings. More than twoscore arrests were reported. Among the meeting places raided by the service men were the People's House....[and] the office of The Call, a Socialist daily."

The demonstrations spurred calls to restrict public activities of left-wing radicals, with Cleveland's city council passing ordinances restricting parades and the display of red flags. The *Salt Lake City Tribune* editorialized, "Free speech has been carried to the point where it is an unrestrained menace."

The May Day riots were followed by a series of race riots in two dozen cities throughout the summer and early fall. Especially violent riots occurred in Washington and Chicago. In

Washington, rumors of the arrest of a black man for rape of a white woman led to four days of mob violence during which groups of white men rioted in the black quarter of the city, attacking random black people on the street. Unlike previous episodes, many blacks fought back against the attacks. When the city finally was brought under control, 10 whites and five blacks were dead.

On July 27, rioting broke out in Chicago in response to the stoning and drowning of a black youth who had drifted into the area of the beaches along Lake Michigan traditionally reserved for whites. The violence lasted 13 days, resulting in 38 fatalities (23 blacks and 15 whites), 537 people were injured, and 1,000 black families were left homeless. It took a militia force of several thousand to restore order.

Alongside the race riots, the fall of 1919 saw labor unrest on a wide scale. On September 9, 1919, Boston police went out on strike to demand higher wages, better working conditions, and recognition of their American Federation of Labor-affiliated union. Governor Calvin Coolidge was forced to dispatch the State Guard to restore order to the city after a couple of nights of lawlessness.

Newspapers around the country labeled the police strike as an expression of the Bolshevist conspiracy, with the *Philadelphia Public Ledger* claiming, "Bolshevism in the United States is no longer a specter. Boston in chaos reveals its sinister substance." Public figures attacked the strikers in similar terms, with Senator Henry Cabot Lodge saying, "If the American Federation of Labor succeeds in getting hold of the police in Boston it will go all over the country, and we shall be in measurable distance of Soviet government by labor unions."

Following the Boston police strike, on September 22, 1919, steel industry union members voted to go on strike, and the strike shut down half the steel industry across the country. The owners, hoping to turn public opinion against the strikers, publicized the radical background of AFL National Committee co-chairman William Z. Foster as indicative that the strike was masterminded by radicals and revolutionaries.

Against this background, Attorney General Palmer struggled to find a mechanism for fighting the "red menace." With the waves of anarchist bombings and racial and labor unrest, Palmer faced pressure from Congress to do something, and in June 1919, he told the House Appropriations Committee that radicals were prepared to "on a certain day...rise up and destroy the government at one fell swoop."

That July, state and federal officers raided an anarchist group in Buffalo, New York, but to Palmer's dismay, a federal judge threw the case out when he found that the anarchists arrested proposed using their free speech rights and not violence to change the government.

Palmer subsequently decided to turn attention to alien radicals, and he became determined to use the existing immigration statutes to deport anarchists, socialists, and communists. To do so, he would need the cooperation of the Secretary of Labor Wilson, who oversaw implementation of the immigration acts. It was Wilson, not Attorney General Palmer, who was authorized to sign arrest warrants and sign deportation orders following a hearing.

The first step was to identify individuals who, because of their immigration status and radical politics, would fall under the statutes. To this end, on August 1 Palmer named a young Department of Justice attorney, J. Edgar Hoover, to head a new division of the Bureau of Investigation. Through the General Investigation Division (often referred to as the Radical Division), Palmer charged Hoover with investigating radical groups and identifying their members. Hoover quickly used his experience at the Library of Congress to develop a detailed process for identifying, indexing, and cross-referencing the names of individuals who could be identified as members of radical organizations. In short order, Hoover and his staff went over lists of subscribers to radical newspapers, membership records, and arrest reports to compile lists of individuals to be subject to deportation proceedings.

Hoover

On the night of November 7, 1919, selected because it was the second anniversary of the Bolshevik Revolution, Palmer launched a series of raids planned by Hoover in over 30 cities targeting the Union of Russian Workers. The largest raid was in New York City, where dozens of plainclothes and uniformed police officers joined federal law enforcement agents in a raid on the "People's House," the headquarters of the Union of Russian Workers. A reporter for the socialist newspaper *New York Call* described it as "one of the most brutal raids ever witnessed in the city."

180 individuals arrested during these raids were among the 249 radicals deported to Russia on December 21, 1919, on the USAT *Buford*. Nicknamed the "Soviet Ark," the ship also carried members of the International Workers of the World and prominent anarchists Emma Goldman and Alexander Berkman, who had been detained earlier for deportation and were not part of the November raid. The *Buford* landed at Hanko, Finland on January 16, 1920, after which the deportees were transported to Petrograd by train.

While Palmer became occupied in November and December 1919 with trying to end the United Mine Worker's coal strike, Hoover worked on organizing subsequent raids. These raids he planned were to be on a much larger scale and target more than one organization. Using the leverage of positive public opinion over the earlier raids, Hoover pressured the Department of Labor into concessions that would result in arrests that cast a much wider net than was possible in the November raids. He persuaded the Labor Department to issue instructions that detainees not be informed of their rights to an attorney until after a case against an individual was established. Hoover, on his own initiative, also broadened the Labor Department's agreement to target members of the Communist Party to include the Communist Labor Party, a completely separate organization. Finally, going against Wilson's insistence that more than merely being a member in a leftist organization was required for a warrant, Hoover found compliant Labor officials willing to issue him the warrants he wanted.

The raids were launched on January 2, 1920, with smaller raids over the next several days and weeks. The raids, which arrested about 3,000 people, included individuals arrested without warrants. Entire organizations were targeted, so the arrests encompassed everyone found in organization meeting halls, which meant the raids picked up members of the organizations who were not radicals, visitors who were not members, and American citizens not eligible for arrest and deportation.

Ultimately, a total of 10,000 suspected radicals were arrested through raids like these over the next several weeks, and the raids proved popular among the frightened public. Most press coverage was positive, with the *Washington Post* editorial entitled "The Red Assassins" being typical in not only applauding the raids but calling on Congress to enact laws enabling Palmer to go further. To those who protested that the raids constituted an infringement on the civil liberties of the radicals, the *Post* article countered, "The right of free speech, printing and assembly in the United States should not include the right to preach bolshevism directly or indirectly. Bolshevism is a declared enemy of the United States and seeks its death. The United States must kill bolshevism or be killed by it. The reds, whether native or alien, who advocate bolshevism, should come within the rigor of the law. There is no time to waste on hairsplitting over infringement of liberty when the enemy is using liberty's weapons for the assassination of liberty."

With the success of the Palmer Raids and the information gathered by Hoover for the Radical Division, it seemed that perhaps the Bureau of Investigation had conquered the anarchist menace. However, although they were publicly confident, both Hoover and Flynn were aware that there were far more anarchists and sympathizers than the raids had identified, and their worst fears would soon be realized.

The Wall Street Bombing

By 1920, horse-drawn wagons were becoming less common on the streets of New York City, replaced by growing numbers of automobiles and trucks. Thus, the few people who noticed the wagon that turned onto Wall Street a little before noon on September 16 remembered it because it seemed particularly dilapidated and the single horse pulling it looked old and tired. At the time, the street was crowded with passers-by and people coming out of offices to begin their lunch break. Given the hustle and bustle, few noticed as the driver of the wagon parked it outside the J.P. Morgan Bank at 23 Wall Street, close to the Stock Exchange and the Sub-Treasury buildings, and then walked briskly away. A few moments later, at 12:01, the wagon exploded.

The blast, whose impact was contained and thus strengthened by the narrow street and tall buildings, was devastating. A column of flame more than 100 feet high boiled into the air, cars were hurled off their wheels, and the buildings themselves seemed to tremble. When the dense, white smoke cleared, it revealed a scene of carnage. Bodies and body parts littered the sidewalks and street, people completely enveloped in flames ran screaming along the street, and blood was splashed up across the walls. A woman's head, still wearing a hat, was visible where it had been blasted into the façade of a building opposite the bank. A hand could be seen balanced on the cornice above the door of the J.P. Morgan Bank. A woman's lower leg and foot, still wearing a shoe, were found on a window sill at the Bankers Trust building. Rescuers rushed to help a woman who had been hurled against the door of the Assay Office by the blast but, when they reached her, they found that she had no arms. The head of the horse that had pulled the wagon was found close to the site, while its hooves were found blocks away, scattered in several directions. Every nearby window was smashed, and many of the occupants were slashed by flying glass. Some ran to the scene to help the injured and the dying, and even more ran away in fear of a second explosion, causing a stampede that injured many others.

Soon, police, firefighters and ambulances began to arrive, and they immediately found more than 30 people dead and many more seriously wounded. Police quickly set up a cordon in front of the J.P. Morgan Bank, which had all of its windows and doors destroyed by the blast.

A modern picture of 23 Wall Street

A picture of the scene shortly after the attack

At first, police believed that the explosion had been an accident, perhaps caused when an automobile had collided with a wagon taking explosives to a nearby building site, but others quickly suspected otherwise. That day, as Flynn was enjoying lunch with a group of friends and colleagues at the Raleigh Hotel in Washington, he was abruptly called from the table to take an urgent telephone call. A few moments later he returned to the table, ashen-faced, telling the members of the group, "What we have expected has happened. New York has been blown up."

Sure enough, when experts from industrial explosives companies and a team of federal detectives who arrived with Flynn arrived at the scene, they quickly concluded that this was no accident. More than 100 pounds of dynamite packed in the center of pieces of loose metal had been detonated with some form of timer, making clear that what happened was a terrorist attack.

The final death toll was 38 people killed, but 146 were seriously injured and hundreds more were lightly injured. The worst damage was done to the J.P. Morgan Bank, where the heavy sash weights that had been packed around the dynamite had pock-marked the façade and smashed in through windows. The damage was left unrepaired as a memorial and can still be seen at 23 Wall Street today. One of the dead was Thomas Joyce, Chief Clerk of the J.P. Morgan Bank, who was struck in the head by shrapnel as he sat at his desk overlooking Wall Street.

Norton Juster's picture of some of the damage still visible on 23 Wall Street

The nearby Stock Exchange was closed soon after the blast, but work crews were pulled in overnight to clear up debris and repair broken windows. The Stock Exchange reopened the following day, and investigators subsequently warned that important evidence might have been lost during the rapid clean up.

On September 17, New York police officers found several printed flyers in a mailbox on Cedar Street, a short distance from Wall Street, and they appeared to have been deposited just before the blast. Printed in dramatic red ink on white paper, they read:

> "Remember, we will not tolerate any longer. Free the political prisoners, or it
> will be sure death for all of you.
>
> American Anarchist Fighters."

It seemed certain that the Wall Street bomb was the work of anarchists, but Flynn was not allowed to take over the investigation due to jurisdiction - the bomb was within the area controlled by the New York City Police Department, so the NYPD would be the primary investigating agency. Flynn was able to use the fact that one of the buildings, the Sub-Treasury and Assay Office, was a federal building, thereby justifying his presence on Wall Street that afternoon. He knew that this would be a high-profile case, and he was keen to ensure that the BOI took control and received any credit that arose from its solution.

The BOI and the NYPD were not the only agencies investigating the blast. Agents of both the Secret Service and the Military Intelligence agency were present on Wall Street that afternoon, and they were joined by a man who had become known in the press as "The Great Detective," a former Secret Service agent named William J. Burns. In 1909, he had founded the William J. Burns International Detective Agency, and Burns had been successful in investigating several high-profile cases, including the 1910 bombing of the *Los Angeles Times* offices by anarchists. The press covered Burns' exploits closely, but by 1920 he had not been involved in any particularly interesting cases for some time. His detective agency had its headquarters just a few blocks from Wall Street, in the Woolworth Building.

Burns

When Burns was spotted on Wall Street poking through the debris within a few hours of the explosion, police demanded to know what he was doing there. He claimed that he was working on behalf of J.P. Morgan Bank, though most people doubted that the bank could have engaged a detective agency so quickly. When police checked this, the bank refused to either confirm or deny that Burns was working for them. It was certainly true that his agency held the contract to provide security for the American Bankers Association, of which J.P. Morgan was a member, but it seems entirely possible that Burns had heard the explosion and, seeing the damage caused by the bomb, quickly decided to make himself part of the investigation.

In the immediate aftermath of the explosion, all of the various people investigating the blast initially struggled to understand what had happened. The eyewitness descriptions and an analysis of the wreckage seemed to confirm that the explosion had originated in a single horse wagon that had been parked outside the J.P. Morgan Bank, so it was on this wagon and its driver that initial investigations focused, but little remained of the wagon. A few pieces of wheel and other wooden parts showing traces of red and yellow paint thought to have been part of the wagon were found, and NYPD detectives appealed to wagon makers and livery stable owners in the city to help identify it. The unfortunate horse that had pulled the wagon had been blown to pieces by the blast - its head and some of the foreparts of its body were found relatively close to the point of detonation, but its rear end and legs had been blasted into fragments. These were carefully collected in the hope that something about the horse, its harnesses, or shoes would prove distinctive enough that someone might recognize them.

A number of similarly sized pieces of metal were recovered from the explosion site and the surrounding area, and these originally baffled detectives. These were a few inches long and with a circular section. Before long, they were recognized as sash weights used in domestic windows. Eventually, it was realized that hundreds of these weights had been packed around what was estimated to have been up to 100 pounds of dynamite on the wagon, creating a deadly hail of red-hot shrapnel when the bomb exploded. These sash weights were found up to five blocks away from Wall Street.

The NYPD put out an appeal for anyone who could "give any information, no matter how slight, regarding any of the details, especially regarding vehicles in the street, which might have caused the explosion, or the presence of any suspicious persons at the time of the explosion." In response, many people came forward, including one or two who were even able to give a description of the driver of the wagon. He had been, they told detectives, "dark-complexioned, unshaven, wiry, probably 35 or 40 years old, and dressed in working clothes and a dark cap. He seemed to be about five feet six inches tall. He had dark hair." That was a fairly detailed description, but there was nothing about it that was sufficiently distinctive to lead to an arrest.

By the end of September 16, all that seemed certain was that the explosion had probably not been caused by an accident involving dynamite bound for a building site. The movement of shipments of dynamite were carefully controlled, and none had been in the center of New York on that day. The discovery the following day of flyers from the American Anarchist Fighters appeared to confirm that this was an act of terrorism, even though there was no way to definitively link the flyers to the explosion.

Of course, the flyers themselves were carefully examined. They had not been professionally printed but produced using rubber stamps, with each letter a separate stamp. Each flyer had been laboriously produced by forming words with the individual letter stamps. Five were found in total, and on most there were misspellings, with the word "remember" being spelled incorrectly on each flyer. However, there was nothing about the flyers to suggest who had printed them and the American Anarchist Fighters were not known to any of the investigating agencies. The assumption was that the driver of the wagon had the flyers in his pocket and dropped them in the mailbox as he walked away, just before the explosion. The mailbox where the flyers were found was a four-minute walk from the site of the explosion.

From the BOI New York office on Park Row, Flynn issued several statements in the days following the explosion. Most of them noted that this was not just an attack on Wall Street and New York City but an attack aimed at the federal government itself. This was important to Flynn, because if this truly was an attack on the federal government, then the BOI was the obvious body to lead the investigation. Behind the scenes, J. Edgar Hoover, now head of the General Intelligence Division, an expanded version of the Radical Division, was combing through records to identify possible suspects.

At the same time, the agents of the William J. Burns International Detective Agency also continued to make enquiries. Newspaper reporters asked Burns again just who he was working for, and he continued to claim his employer was the J.P. Morgan Bank. However, when the same reporters asked the bank to confirm this, they were met with a denial. Undaunted, Burns offered a reward of over $500 for information leading to the arrest of the perpetrators within days of the explosion.

In response, the NYPD offered a $10,000 reward for information that led to a conviction, and NYPD detectives continued to sift through the physical evidence retrieved from the scene. Within days they were able to announce that the wagon on which the bomb had been carried to Wall Street was a delivery wagon "of one or one and a half tons capacity, about 10 to 15 years old." It had been painted red, black, and white, and the horse pulling it was at least 20-years- old. The horse had been reshod a short time before its death, so NYPD detectives tried to find the blacksmith responsible.

Despite the frantic work being done by the NYPD, it was the BOI that made the first arrest in this case. The Bureau learned that at least three people who worked in the Financial District had been sent letters advising them to avoid that area on Wednesday because of an unspecified threat of some form of attack by a "Bolshevik." The explosion had taken place on Thursday, not Wednesday, but it seemed that the writer of the letters must have had some knowledge of an impending attack.

Oddly enough, the writer of the letter was Edwin P. Fischer, a tennis player who had won the mixed doubles title at the U.S. National Championships four times between 1894 and 1898. Fischer had no known connection with anarchists or any form of radical politics, but the warnings he had given also could not be ignored. He was in Canada, apparently for a tennis tournament, and the authorities there were instructed to hold him until BOI agents could bring him to New York for questioning.

Fischer

When he arrived in New York City, Fischer quickly proved to be, at the very least, eccentric. He was wearing three sets of clothes – two suits on top of a full set of tennis whites – which he claimed was done intentionally so that he did not have to take luggage with him. According to Fischer, he always wore his tennis gear under outer clothes so that he could be ready to play tennis "at a moment's notice." When questioned about the bomb, he explained that he had received the warning "from God and through the air."

It turned out that this was not the first time that Fischer had warned friends and colleagues about impending disasters or Bolshevik attacks, but it was the first time that he came close to being accurate. After questioning, it was determined that Fischer had absolutely no knowledge of the bombing, and his family agreed to have him admitted to the psychiatric ward of Amityville Asylum in New York "for his own safety."

The NYPD soon made an arrest, and this time the suspect was a known radical named Alexander Brailovsky, a Russian émigré and the publisher of the radical Communist newssheet *Russky Golos*. The evidence against Brailovsky amounted to a claim by one witness that he had been seen on Wall Street within half an hour of the explosion and that he appeared to be laughing. He was released without charges when NYPD could find no firm evidence to link him with the Wall Street blast or anarchist groups.

To William Flynn and the investigators of the BOI, it seemed virtually certain that the Wall Street bombing had been conducted by an anarchist group, but nobody had heard of the American Anarchist Fighters and no other group claimed responsibility for the attack. As weeks and then months passed without the identification of a viable suspect, the investigation became a matter of looking at known anarchist groups and trying to identify which one might have mounted the attack.

In November 1920, Senator Warren G. Harding of Ohio defeated Democratic Governor James M. Cox of Ohio in the presidential election. Harding ran a campaign centered on the slogan "return to normalcy," which found resonance with a country on the brink of recession and weary of violence and terror. Harding won a landslide victory, and a new administration meant there would be a new Attorney General. On March 4, 1921, Harry Daugherty was appointed as Attorney General and inherited control of the Bureau of Investigation. A. Mitchell Palmer retired from office and spent his remaining years practicing law and participating in Democratic politics, including supporting Franklin Delano Roosevelt in 1932. He died on May 11, 1936 in Washington from cardiac complications following an appendectomy.

Ironically, the man most intimately associated with the Palmer Raids today was not its namesake, and his career arc went quite differently. If Hoover had initially been worried about his future career with Palmer gone, it turned out he had little reason to be, because incoming Attorney General Daugherty was pleased to find that the files of Hoover's Radical Division contained information on Harding's political opponents as well as radicals. In fact, thanks to his reputation as a nonpartisan bureaucrat who would carry out his superior's instructions without question, Hoover was able to get the job he really wanted: Assistant Chief of the Bureau of Investigation.

For a time, things continued as before. The BOI continued to focus on looking at anarchist groups, mainly using information provided by J. Edgar Hoover and the General Intelligence Division. The NYPD investigation seemed to run out of steam and no further arrests were made after the release of Alexander Brailovsky.

In the William J. Burns International Detective Agency, the focus was on Communists rather than anarchist suspects. One man in particular, Ludwig Martens, became their main suspect. Martens arrived in America in 1916, and in 1919 he was ordered by Lenin to set up a Soviet diplomatic office in New York City. He did this, establishing an office in the World Tower Building and hiring a number of well-known American Socialists. Naturally, since American troops were still occupying parts of Siberia and fighting the Red Army, the administration of President Wilson refused to formally recognize the new office, and William Burns and others believed that Martens' real role was to fund and encourage a Communist revolution in America.

Martens was called before a Senate Judiciary Committee and admitted receiving funds from Moscow, but he denied that these were used for anything but raising the profile of Communism in America. By January 1921, there were moves to begin deportation proceedings against Martens, but, before these were complete, Martens and his family left America on a ship bound for Russia. To William Burns, this looked like a guilty man fleeing before he could be arrested. Burns immediately sent William Linde, a former member of the Communist Party in America who had acted as an informer for the Burns International Detective Agency, to Moscow to continue to gather evidence against Martens.

In the BOI, the focus remained on anarchist suspects. A few days before the Wall Street bombing, two Italian-American anarchists, Nicola Sacco and Bartolomeo Vanzetti, had been indicted for first-degree murder and armed robbery following the death of two payroll guards at the Slater-Morrill Shoe Company factory in Braintree, Massachusetts. The Sacco-Vanzetti case had attracted a great deal of press interest, and BOI investigators wondered whether these could be the "political prisoners" mentioned in the flyer associated with the Wall Street bombing.

It was clear that neither Sacco nor Vanzetti could be suspects in the Wall Street bombing since both had been in prison when it happened, but Flynn believed that they might know something about who had carried out the attack. However, despite an intensive investigation, which included infiltrating an undercover BOI informer into Sacco's prison cell, the BOI could not uncover any direct evidence of a connection between Sacco and Vanzetti and the Wall Street bomb. The BOI did investigate Aldino Felicani, an Italian-America anarchist who was raising funds to help pay for Sacco and Vanzetti's defense, but again, this did not yield any direct connection with the Wall Street bombing.

For his part, Hoover identified three separate but connected anarchist groups that were believed to be operating within the United States. Pro Prensa was a group of mainly Spanish anarchists believed to be based in Philadelphia and New York. L'Era Nuova was based in New Jersey and comprised mainly of Italian-Americans. However, both these groups had been infiltrated by BOI agents and many of their members were deported in early 1920 following the Palmer raids.

The largest anarchist group was one headed by Luigi Galleani. This also mainly comprised Italian-Americans and had its headquarters in Boston. Although it was never proved, Flynn believed that this group had been behind many of the bombs planted in 1919, and while Luigi Galleani was deported from America in July 1920, many other members of the group he had formed remained in America. From the beginning, Flynn focused the efforts of the BOI on members of Galleani's anarchist group. Within days of the explosion, he told reporters that he believed that the Wall Street bombing was the work of the same people who had carried out anarchist bombings in 1919, the "Galleanisti."

This investigation was not easy. Almost all the members of this group were Italian-Americans, but the BOI had only three agents who could speak Italian. In conjunction with that, Hoover had the names and addresses of virtually everyone who had ever subscribed to an anarchist newsletter in America, which amounted to over 2,000 people. The problem was tracking them down and proving that they had a connection with any form of political violence.

An early suspect was Giuseppe Sberna, a New York anarchist with connections to the Galleanisti. When agents discovered that he was described as dark-complexioned, dark-haired and of medium height and build (close to the description given by witnesses who had seen the man who parked the wagon on Wall Street), they were even more interested. An elaborate scheme was developed in which BOI agents posing as sellers of an anarchist newspaper went to his New York City apartment. There, his puzzled wife explained that Sberna had returned to Italy in early 1920 fearing deportation following the Palmer Raids.

The BOI was also interested in Gaetano Caruso, a young Italian-American who had been arrested for his part in an armed robbery of a poker game in September 1920. A police raid on his house revealed anarchist literature and communication from members of the Galleanisti. Flynn visited Caruso in prison in October 1920 and was initially optimistic, writing to the Attorney General, "I am of the opinion that he will soon consent to make a statement that will aid us materially." His optimism proved unfounded, and Caruso never provided any useful information.

The ongoing BOI investigation eventually identified a man who seemed to be the most promising suspect to date: Vincenzo Leggio, an immigrant from Palermo who was a known anarchist and was said to look like the man seen by witnesses parking the wagon on Wall Street. The problem was that no one knew where Vincenzo Leggio could be located; military intelligence suggested that Leggio had been deported in June 1919, and an informant was confident that Leggio had left America in early 1920 to return to Sicily. Conversely, others were equally confident that Leggio was staying with anarchist friends in New England or traveling in Canada raising funds for the anarchist cause. BOI agents spent a great deal of time looking for Leggio, but they failed to find him.

Then, on April 19, 1921, police in Scranton, Pennsylvania arrested an Italian-American anarchist named Tito Ligi on charges of draft evasion. Flynn was exultant, believing that Tito Ligi was actually Vincenzo Leggio. The arrest of Tito Ligi was an important development because it suggested that the BOI had been successful, and it seemed to verify the need for the kind of information maintained by Hoover in identifying and rounding up anarchists as part of the Palmer Raids. The arrest gave the impression that the BOI knew all about anarchist groups in the United States, and since most people believed that the Wall Street bombing was the work of an anarchist group, there was an expectation amongst the general public and even members of the government that the BOI would quickly identify the perpetrators.

When they failed to do so, however, people began to question the efficiency of the BOI and the ability of its leader, Flynn. When Flynn cautiously told the press about the arrest of Ligi, he was careful to avoid saying directly that this person had been involved in the Wall Street bombing, but that was what was reported anyway. The headline in the *New York Sun*, for example, read: "Federal Agents Think Wall Street Plot Cleared."

Initial investigations did suggest that Ligi was a viable suspect, and when police raided his apartment, they found two pistols, anarchist flyers and letters from other known anarchists. When questioned, Ligi claimed that he could not remember where he had been during the first half of September 1920. Flynn had a photograph of Ligi taken, and this was shown to witnesses who had seen the man who parked the wagon on Wall Street just before the explosion. Two thought he might be the man they had seen, while two others were not sure.

Reporters claimed that Ligi had been living during September 1920 in a dilapidated building above an abandoned mine, a place that had been used for years as an anarchist hideout. Police investigated and found in a back room a number of sash weights that were identical to those used in the Wall Street bomb.

Overall, Ligi seemed the best suspect to date, but there were some worrying discrepancies; most witnesses had described the man who had parked the wagon on Wall Street as of medium height and with a dark moustache. Ligi was tall and clean-shaven. There was also the still unresolved question of whether Tito Ligi was actually Vincenzo Leggio.

When the case finally began to make its way through the courts in April 1921, the case against Ligi fell apart. Only one witness was willing to place Ligi at Wall Street at the time of the bombing, while the other witnesses were either not certain or were sure that Ligi had not been there. His defense team produced more than 15 witnesses who testified that Ligi had been in New Jersey on September 16. Moreover, the BOI could produce no evidence that Ligi was Vincenzo Leggio, and several witnesses swore that he was not. Ligi was eventually sentenced to one year in prison for draft evasion, which at least gave BOI agents more time to look into the case, but they were unable to find any evidence to link Ligi with the Wall Street bomb.

In May 1921, BOI agents made another arrest. Giuseppe De Filippis was an Italian-American living in the city of Bayonne in New Jersey. BOI agents had been watching De Filippis for some time and at least one eyewitness had placed this suspect at Wall Street moments before the explosion, talking to Tito Ligi. De Filippis was charged with "exploding a bomb in the street and immediately in front of the United States Assay Office." He appeared before a federal court on May 31 but was released shortly after due to a complete lack of evidence against him.

More than eight months after the Wall Street explosion, it seemed that Flynn and the BOI were not actually close to finding the people responsible for the bombing. On August 21, 1921, Flynn was abruptly dismissed from his position as head of the Bureau of Investigation. He was allowed to tell the press that he was resigning to take up another job offer, but most understood that his failure to find the suspect or suspects behind the Wall Street bomb had fatally undermined his position.

After being forced to retire from the Bureau, William Flynn founded his own detective agency in New York City, but this was obviously on a very small scale compared to the larger agencies. Flynn also wrote scenarios for the emerging motion picture industry and edited a popular pulp magazine, *Flynn's Weekly Detective Fiction*, before dying of a heart attack in 1928.

In Flynn's place, Attorney General Daugherty announced the appointment of none other than William J. Burns as the BOI's new director. Burns just so happened to be a personal friend of Daugherty's, and J. Edgar Hoover was elevated to a new position as Burns' deputy.

Under Burns, the BOI investigation would turn in a completely new direction, ignoring American anarchists and looking instead at Russian-backed Communists. By this time, Burns was frustrated that he had not heard from William Linde for several months after Linde was sent to Russia to investigate the case against Ludwig Martens. He sent another man, German-born Paul Altendorf, to Russia to find Linde. Altendorf sent a couple of positive messages from Poland claiming that the Wall Street bombing was solved and that Martens was the man behind it, but then he also disappeared. In October, Burns sent a BOI agent, Sylvester Cosgrove, to Poland to try to find both men. Cosgrove was able to track down both men and in November sent Burns a terse message that read, "If story true, matter solved. Doubt it."

In December, Polish authorities arrested William Linde, and once again, American newspapers carried headlines that suggested that the Wall Street bomber had been found. Burns did nothing to undermine this story, claiming that BOI agent Cosgrove had been instrumental in betraying Linde to the Poles. For a very short time, Burns was lauded, but it was eventually revealed that Linde had been an agent in the employ of the Burns Detective Agency. Burns admitted this, but he claimed that he had always suspected that Linde was really the bomber and that his employment was a ruse to enable the agency to track Linde. It rapidly transpired that there was no evidence at all to link Linde with the Wall Street bombing, and Burns' involvement with Linde looked, to most people, very odd indeed.

Linde was released by the Polish authorities and continued to correspond with Burns, who maintained his belief that Communists were behind the Wall Street bombing. A BOI raid on a Communist Party meeting led to several arrests, but no convictions. Membership in the Communist Party was not illegal, and, despite what Burns thought, there was no evidence that Communists had ever advocated for or supported acts of terrorism.

In May 1923, BOI agents arrested the last major suspect in the Wall Street bombing: Noah Lerner, a 23-year-old electrician who was also a member of the Communist Party and who had recently returned from Russia, where he had spent time in the international colony at Kuzbas. Once again, the newspaper headlines were triumphant, but a week later, Lerner was released. There was simply no evidence against him, and he was able to provide an alibi for his whereabouts on September 16, 1920.

In early 1924, Burns was forced to resign as Director of the Bureau of Investigation due to a series of shady deals undertaken with his friend, Attorney General Daugherty. Burns retired to Sarasota, Florida after being ousted, and he became a regular contributor to magazines with accounts of true crime cases that he had been involved in. He died in 1932 after suffering several heart attacks, and his sons inherited the Burns International Detective Agency and built it into one of the largest and most successful investigative agencies in America.

Thanks to Hoover's reputation and seemingly straightlaced morals, he was able to avoid the charges of corruption that tarred Burns and another Bureau of Investigation agent, Gaston Means. The Harding Administration was riven with scandals, and the Justice Department was no different. After Harding's sudden death and Calvin Coolidge's assumption of the presidency, Daugherty, Burns, and Means were all removed from office, tried on various corruption charges, and convicted. This left Hoover as the highest ranking official of the Bureau of Investigation.

New Attorney General Harlan Fiske Stone had been a harsh critic of the Palmer Raids, but Stone, who had to know of Hoover's role in the raids, nevertheless took the advice of both Assistant Secretary of Commerce Lawrence Ritchey and Assistant Attorney General Mabel Willebrant when they recommended Hoover as the new Chief of the Bureau of Investigation. Stone offered Hoover the job of Acting Director, but Hoover recalled later making several conditions of his acceptance of the position: "The Bureau must be divorced from politics and not be a catch-all for political hacks. Appointments must be based on merit. Secondly, promotions will be made on proven ability and the Bureau will be responsible only to the Attorney General."

Stone agreed, and on May 10, 1924, J. Edgar Hoover became Acting Director of the Bureau of Investigation. He would hold the position for the next 48 years, and in the process he became one of the longest serving and most powerful civil servants in American history.

The Legacy of the Attack

Over the coming years, many other suspects were subsequently identified as potentially being involved with the bombing, but none were even remotely credible.

In March 1924, Ralph Thurber, then a prisoner being held in Pentonville Prison in England, announced that he knew the names of all the people involved in the Wall Street bombing. These were a colorful crew who sounded as if they belonged to a pulp magazine story, including Big Jeff, The Kid, and the inevitable moll, Girlie O'Day. Almost unbelievably, the BOI spent time investigating this claim and concluded that none of these people actually existed. To the surprise of few, it simply turned out that Ralph Thurber was an "awful liar."

In February the following year, Thurber's friend, Herbert Wilson, then a prisoner in San Quentin, admitted selling a large quantity of nitroglycerine to a group he believed were the Wall Street bombers. Weary agents were once again detailed to investigate, and they quickly concluded that Wilson's claim was "bunk."

In October 1925, a man named Richard O'Hara confessed to NYPD detectives that he was the wagon driver. After a short investigation, O'Hara was sent to the psychiatric wing of Bellevue Hospital and treated for psychosis related to acute alcoholism.

In 1930, the BOI received several letters from Harry Brant, a former undercover operative who claimed that the Wall Street bombing had been carried out by an unnamed detective agency. In 1934, a man named Stephen Doyle wrote a series of letters to the BOI claiming that the bomb had been part of a plot cooked up by J.P. Morgan and William Burns (aided by Flynn) to discredit the Communist Party in America. Neither of these claims were credible, and they were not investigated in detail.

During World War II, the FBI conducted one final investigation into the bombing. This was prompted by a claim in 1944 that the bomb had involved Japanese engineers, but no evidence was found to support this theory, and a review of all the available evidence led only to a statement that that the original investigation had involved scrutinizing several radical political groups: "Such as the Union of Russian Workers, the I.W.W., Communist, etc. and from the result of the investigations to date it would appear that none of the aforementioned organizations had any hand in the matter and that the explosion was the work of either Italian anarchists or Italian terrorists."

Another suspect was revealed not by official investigators but by author Professor Paul Avrich in his 1991 book about Sacco and Vanzetti. The man named by Avrich was Mario Buda, an Italian-American anarchist who was a follower of Galleani and a close friend of both Sacco and Vanzetti. Buda was certainly believed by police to have been involved in earlier anarchist bombings, though he was never charged with any. The Wall Street bombing took place within days of the indictment of Sacco and Vanzetti. Buda is believed to have been living in New York City at the time and left America soon after the Wall Street explosion. He returned to Italy, where he dropped his support for anarchism and became a fervent supporter of Mussolini and the fascists.

This is a plausible theory, but the evidence used to support it is entirely circumstantial. A search of BOI files has failed to locate a single mention of Mario Buda. No member of an anarchist group in America named Buda as the bomber at the time or subsequently. Avrich's contention that Buda was the bomber comes from unnamed sources and from hints dropped later by Buda and members of his family that he was the bomber. That is not impossible, but it is far from proven.

Other theories have suggested that the bombing was not a terrorist attack at all, but a bungled attempt to rob the Federal Reserve Bank. Flynn and others seem to have assumed that it was an anarchist attack because it followed a number of other anarchist bombs, but there was no proven link between the bomb and the flyers from the American Anarchist Fighters that were found the following day. It also seems very odd that no anarchist group ever tried to claim responsibility for the most notorious act of terrorism in the U.S. at the time.

Those who assert the bombing was part of a plot to rob the bank suggest that the bomb was planted to destroy or damage the Sub-Treasury Building, where a gold reserve worth millions of dollars was being held that day. Perhaps the robbers hoped to use the confusion following the blast to mount a raid on the bank and believed that it would be blamed on terrorists. Like several other theories, this is at least plausible, but no direct evidence has ever been found to support it, and there was no attempt to rob the bank in the aftermath of the explosion.

Finally, there is a theory that the explosion was actually nothing more than a terrible accident. New York City was experiencing a building boom in the 1920s, and dynamite was regularly used for demolition. The movement of consignments of dynamite was tightly controlled, but there was also known to be a lively clandestine trade in dynamite. Could the very earliest theory, that an automobile collided with a parked wagon loaded with dynamite and set off the explosion, be true?

It seems unlikely that anyone will ever know with complete certainty exactly what happened on Wall Street on September 16, 1920, but anarchist bombings certainly continued. In April 1927, Sacco and Vanzetti were sentenced to death, and weeks later, a mail bomb addressed to Massachusetts Governor Alvan T. Fuller was intercepted. In August, there were mass protests and a strike, and on August 5 bombs exploded in Baltimore, Philadelphia and on the New York Subway. On May 18, 1928, a bomb destroyed the front porch of the home of state executioner Robert Elliott. In 1932, the home of Judge Thayer, the man who had sentenced Sacco and Vanzetti to death, was partially destroyed by a massive bomb.

However, by the 1930s support for anarchism was dwindling in America. Communism and fascism had become the most important new political movements in the world, and neither had any place for anarchists who believed in a state-free world. The movement led from Stalin's Soviet Union was the most important revolutionary political force in the world, and anarchists were brutally repressed inside of the Soviet Union. Outside of it, anarchist movements were deliberately undermined and suppressed by the Communists.

Meanwhile, new immigration policies in the United States were deliberately targeted at countries that were regarded as centers of anarchism. Strict quotas and checks were applied to immigrants coming from Italy, the main source of American anarchism, and the Soviet Union, while quotas for immigrants from "safe countries" such as France and the United Kingdom, were increased. Support for groups such as the Industrial Workers of the World dwindled until by the

1930s, the anarchist movement had ceased to be a major factor in American politics. Ironically, the anarchist attacks that government officials had tirelessly tried to connect to Communists were essentially put to an end by the rise in popularity of Communism itself.

With that, the Bureau of Investigation fundamentally changed. Its earliest leaders (Finch, Flynn, and Burns) were traditional detectives who shaped the Bureau into something resembling a traditional detective agency, but with Hoover at the helm, it became something quite different. Hoover had always believed in the power of information, and he concentrated on amassing information to fight gangsters, Nazis, and Communists. Hoover became immensely powerful, in part because many politicians were terrified of the information he might have on them.

The Wall Street bombing itself would remain the deadliest terrorist attack in American history until a bomb planted by Timothy McVeigh destroyed the Alfred P. Murrah Federal Building in Oklahoma City and killed 166 people in 1995, nearly 75 years later. However, the Wall Street bombing is now largely forgotten. There is no memorial to those who died on that day, and the only visible reminder in New York City is the limestone façade of 23 Wall Street.

This is ironic because many of the political issues that created the atmosphere in which the Wall Street attack occurred still persist a century later. Marx's *Communist Manifesto* did help inspire a series of revolutions in the 20th century, most notably in Russia and China, but the atrocities of leaders in those countries seemingly did a great deal to discredit the assertion that socialist revolution would end conflict and exploitation. Whether the *Manifesto*'s calls for a "dictatorship of the proletariat" are to blame for these and other brutal acts committed by communist regimes remains a topic of charged debate.

Meanwhile, the demise of the Soviet Union and the recent embrace of capitalism by the nominally socialist People's Republic of China have for many observers largely discredited both Marx's political prescriptions and his economic analyses. By the end of the 20th century, sociologists openly asked whether capitalism had the contradictions Marx identified or succeeded in closing them. For example, Axel van den Berg asserted that modern capitalism "has managed to avert, without changing its fundamental characteristics, practically all the consequences which Marx predicted would result from the basic contradiction between the forces and the relations of production… there is no independent evidence, apart from Marx's word, to support the claim that capitalism remains contradiction ridden." Instead, as economist Ernest Van Den Haag argued, "contrary to Marx' prediction, the 'misery of the workers' has not increased. On the contrary, their living standards have risen more, and more rapidly than those of the middle and upper classes."

On the other hand, the financial crisis of 2008 and current trends such as declining wages, endemic unemployment, and prolonged recession have revived interest in Communism's account of the inevitable stratification of classes and the intrinsically self-destructive trajectory of capitalism. While history has clearly not proceeded according to the predictions advanced in the

Communist Manifesto or desired by the anarchists, a number of its central ideas are likely to remain under discussion as long as the contradictions of global capitalism persist.

Online Resources

Other 20ᵗʰ century history titles by Charles River Editors

Other titles about the Wall Street Bombing on Amazon

Bibliography

Avrich, Paul (1996). Sacco and Vanzetti: The Anarchist Background. Princeton University Press. ISBN 978-0-691-02604-6.

Gage, Beverly (2009). The Day Wall Street Exploded: A Story of America in Its First Age of Terror. New York: Oxford University Press. ISBN 978-0-19-514824-4. OCLC 779913767.

Larabee, Ann (2015). "Sabotage". The Wrong Hands: Popular Weapons Manuals and Their Historic Challenges to a Democratic Society. New York: Oxford University Press.

McCormick, Charles H. (2005). Hopeless Cases: The Hunt for the Red Scare Terrorist Bombers. Lanham, Maryland: University Press of America. ISBN 978-0-7618-3132-7. OCLC 60358652.

Neville, John F. (2004). 20th-Century Cause Cèlébre: Sacco, Vanzetti, and the Press, 1920–1927. Westport, Connecticut: Praeger. ISBN 978-0-275-97783-2. OCLC 54350494.

Pernicone, Nunzio (2003). "War among the Italian Anarchists: The Galleanisti's Campaign against Carlo Tresca". In Cannistraro, Philip V.; Meyer, Gerald (eds.). The Lost World of Italian American Radicalism: Politics, Labor, and Culture. Westport, Connecticut: Praeger. pp. 77–98. ISBN 978-0-275-97891-4. OCLC 52335014.

Wellbrook, Christopher (2009). "Seething with the Ideal: Galleanisti and Class Struggle in Late 19th-Century and Early 20th-Century USA". WorkingUSA.

Free Books by Charles River Editors

We have brand new titles available for free most days of the week. To see which of our titles are currently free, click on this link.

Discounted Books by Charles River Editors

We have titles at a discount price of just 99 cents everyday. To see which of our titles are currently 99 cents, click on this link.

CPSIA information can be obtained
at www.ICGtesting.com
Printed in the USA
LVHW061614210920
666683LV00011B/899